ALSO BY EVAN THOMAS

THE VERY BEST MEN:
Four Who Dared: The Early Years of the CIA

THE MAN TO SEE:
Edward Bennett Williams
Ultimate Insider; Legendary Trial Lawyer

THE WISE MEN:
Six Friends and the World They Made
(with Walter Isaacson)

Evan Thomas

A TOUCHSTONE BOOK
PUBLISHED BY SIMON & SCHUSTER
NEW YORK • LONDON • TORONTO • SYDNEY